HOW TO BE FUNNY
WHEN YOU OWE
MONEY!

by

David Samson
funnyguy.com

Illustrated by
Jack Medoff

SPECIALIST PRESS INTERNATIONAL

New York

DEDICATION:

To All Those To Whom I Owe More Than I Can Possibly Repay!

How To Be Funny When You Owe Money

Published by

The Funny Guy Company

and

COPYRIGHT © 2009 DAVID SAMSON

BOOK DESIGN, COVER DESIGN BY MARTIN ARCHER
COVER TYPE DESIGN BY DENISE LABELLE
ILLUSTRATIONS BY JACK MEDOFF

ISBN: 978-156171-216-8
Library of Congress Cataloging
in-Publication Data
Samson, David
How To Be Funny When
You Owe Money

For any
additional information, visit:
www. FunnyGuy.com
and
www.spibooks.com
or contact:
publicity@spibooks.com
dave@funnyguy.com

THE FUNNYGUY.COM LIBRARY:
Available from bookstores everywhere!
(see book descriptions and ordering info at back of book)

How To Get God To Return Your Calls

The Joy of Depression

Men Who Hate Themselves:
(And The Women Who Agree With Them)

Wake Up And Smell The Coffin

American Idle

The O'Really Factor

Do Reality Checks Ever Bounce?

Masturbation for Morons

Useless Knowledge [1]

The Official Millennium Survival Handbook [2]

Is He For Real? [3]

Is He Mr. Right? [3]

The Middle Age of Aquarius

Love Codes [3]

1001 Ways You Reveal Your Personality [3]

1001 More Ways You Reveal Your Personality [3]

Par ents Who Stay Lovers [3]

Rob Parr's Post-Pregnancy Workout [4]

Tammy Faye: Telling It My Way [5]

SAY YOUR PURRS! - 99 Ways To Misuse A Cat

1. With Joe Edelman
2. With Peter Bergman (of The Fire Sign Theatre)
3. With Dr. Elayne Kahn 4. With Rob Parr
5. With Tammy Faye Bakker

TABLE OF CONTENTS

CHAPTER ONE

The Credit You Don't Deserve

The phone rings. It rings again. Again and again and again and AGAIN! The knot in your stomach tightens. Your palms break out in sweat. You've heard that voice on your answering machine before. Not once, not twice. But dozens of times. That same voice. A voice that means business. A voice that says you've got until the end of the day. A voice that says there's a decision about to be made about YOU! There's no doubt about it. This voice is determined to terrorize you for the rest your sorry DEBT-RIDDEN life. But whose voice is it?

Well, it's certainly not the voice that seduced you with ZERO interest. It's not the voice that promised you NO payments for the next twelve months. It's not the voice that claimed the rate was adjustable but would PROBABLY never go over 2%.

And of course, it's not the voice they used in hundreds of offers and solicitations for things you would have never dreamt of buying in a million years except for the fact that they gave you CREDIT!

That's right, my frind. You were pre-approved. PRE-AP-PROVED! That's way better than folks who were just approved. You were approved even before you were approved and you definitely approved of that. You were a premiere customer, you had an excellent credit rating, you had been highly recommended, you were part of a select few, indeed you were ready to claim the credit that you DESERVED!!

And boy did you deserve more credit. For you had already run out of the credit you already had. You had maxed out every single one of your 46 credit cards including the one from Wal-Marts. There were seven years of payments left on your Plasma TV. After getting financing for your BMW, you barely had enough left over for a six pack of Bud. But still you paid your bills by the DUE DATE.

Oh yes, what a great credit risk you were! They practically BEGGED you to transfer your current balance to their bank card. They pointed out what a moron you were for NOT getting a home equity loan. They were kind enough to extend your car payments until the year 2017. And what made you worthy of all this virtually limitless cash being thrown in your lap?

You were a dumb sap. And they just had to wait -- wait until you finally OVEREXTENDED yourself, until you reached the cosmic limits of your credit universe. Oh yes my friend, as the bills went out like clockwork, they waited for you just like they had waited for millions of other schmucks. Just waiting for the right moment to STRIKE!

Hitting you with late charges, rate hikes, over-the-limit fees and penalties as you struggled valiantly to make the monthly minimum payments. Make no mistake. They intentionally sabotaged your credit rating by ungracefully reducing your grace period again and again. They knew that male or female they had you by the nuts, so tightly that even the Mafia's credit terms seemed merciful!

Small wonder it wasn't long before -- under the staggering weight of a mountain of debts which could have easily financed a fleet of aircraft carriers -- you fell JUST A LITTLE BEHIND in your payments. And then, in a mere millisecond, your smug illusion of credit worthiness was shattered forever. In almost no time they went after you big time, hitting you with every high pressure collection tactic under the sun.

To start off with, "Customer Service" people calling you every minute of the day including Sunday saying that your account was now definitely OVERDUE. Next countless warnings from their billing departments stating your account was about to be CANCELLED.

After which numerous threats to turn your account over to COLLECTION agencies. Followed by calls from collection agencies. Then doomsday messages from those same firms declaring that they were turning your deadbeat ass over to LAWYERS. Finally calls from lawyers. More calls from more lawyers. Calls which you completely ignored until --

They served you with a SUMMONS! Those sneaky little SOB's. You'd been successfully dodging them for months and here, smack dab in the middle of waxing your BMW, you get served. You stare at it over and over. It's definitely an official court document and you are definitely the defendant -- except you have no defense!

There's even a TRIAL DATE!

Let's face it, pal. You're screwed!

They're going to get a JUDGMENT against you. In fact, they're going to get fifteen judgments against you. But that's okay, at least there's a sure way out. You can always declare BANKRUPTCY!

Oh yeah? Dream on, you moron! Just remember these same clowns have passed the new bankruptcy law. That's right. Could you even qualify to have your debts wiped clean and make a fresh start? Oh yes, you're trembling by now. You're consumed with anxiety.

So you decide to run down and see a bankruptcy lawyer. Except when hand him your Visa card, he throws that platinum plastic back in your face. Cash only, you sorry pathetic LOSER!

Yes, it's a sad commentary. As they let you charge up a storm, you let them take CHARGE of your life. You let them intimidate you. Living in constant fear and denial, you avoided dealing with them until it was too late. Then it came. In a final act of total humiliation, you begged for sympathy as they snickered to themselves!

You told them over and over about the medical bills which were piling up for your Chihuahua. You told them how you lost your job as a valet at McDonald's. You even revealed that you were schizophrenic and that it was really your OTHER self which ordered all those items from Victoria's Secret.

The bottom line is you tried to play it straight. You tried to do the right thing. You tried to meet your fiscal OBLIGATIONS. And where did it get you? Right to the end of your rope. Because all along they were setting you up. Subjecting you to their stupefying stipulations, which were cleverly hidden in small print on the back of your monthly statements.

There's no doubt about it.

They drove you totally and absolutely crazy. So now is the time to drive them totally and absolutely CRAZY. Now is the time to make them dance to your tune. Now is the time to get finally even with them for what they've done to your life. Get the picture!? Now is the time to reclaim your phone as your own. And youvv can be fully assured, it's a lot easier and much more fun than you ever dreamed possible!

CHAPTER TWO

Become A Total Phoney Now!

Right at your fingertips, you have the MOST powerful weapon ever conceived for dealing with blood-sucking creditors. What's even better, you have at least two or three of them in your home, probably several more in your car or purse. It's your PHONE! And by using our foolproof scripts and special sound effects (available on CD or free at www.funnyguy.com/sfx), your phone will make you virtually INVINCIBLE when dealing with scummy banks or collection agencies, no matter what time they call!

How ironic. They believe your phone is THEIR weapon, but you're going to turn the tables on them. Think about it. On the phone, you can say anything you want, play any type of sound you want, and in process pretend to be anything you want. You are absolutely under NO OBLIGATION to be straightforward and honest with these leeches and parasites.

What's even better, technology has made it easier to yank their collective chains with caller ID, call forwarding, multiple lines, and don't forget that biggest boon of all -- the cell phone!

Nevertheless, you may be feeling slightly guilty about using the phone to become a total PHONEY. Well, forget about it! These bill collectors are lying to you the moment they open their sub-moronic mouths. Will they tell you their ACTUAL names? Where THEY live? What their Social Security numbers are? And how much they really OWE? We don't think so! They're used to setting all the rules and therefore you're entitled to make them total fools!

Here's how to have fun with these clowns. Using our special sound effects, you're going to create your own SONIC REALITY and suck those cretins right in. They won't have a clue what's going on! And best of all, there's practically nothing to it. That's because your phone only produces sounds. Think of all the different sounds you hear each day, from birds chirping to your spouse farting.

Now imagine a creditor calling and suddenly hearing a UFO abducting you, a police car chasing you, or a wolf pack devouring you. Envision a creditor believing you're a CIA-obsessed nut, in the middle of an orgy, or screaming at your eleven adopted children from Bangla Desh. With some luck, it might just give those colossal jerk-offs a well-deserved migraine!

To set the stage and get you into the mood, you'll have dozens of customized sound effects at your immediate disposal. From the plausible to the absurd, you'll be able to stop any creditor in their tracks as they wonder what the hell is happening on your end.

We'll show you exactly what to say as the sound effects play. It's way better than therapy. The professionally mastered tracks do all the work for you. As a matter of fact, the toughest thing will be stopping yourself from cracking up as your creditors go NUTS!

Imagine never feeling intimidated by them again. For with this hilarious program you're totally in control. In almost no time, you'll master the basics and move forward to more advanced strategies.

Have a party. Invite friends over as you put creditors on the speaker phone and pretend to be attacked by Zombies, aboard a nuclear submarine, or hooked up in a hospital emergency room. But make sure everyone stays quiet -- you don't want to give the joke away!

There's no doubt about it. Driving your creditors crazy is the SANEST way to handle all those collection calls. Now whenever they demand their money, all you have to do is act funny. That's right. Gone forever are the days when bill collectors used to abuse you. Because from this day forward they'll only do one thing --

Amuse you!

CHAPTER THREE

Give Me Liberty Or Give Me Debt!

Americans are over 11,000,000,000,000 (11 trillion) dollars in debt. Divide that by the current census bureau population figure of 295,734,134 to ascertain the average national household debt and you'll fry your damn calculator just like we did!

Indeed, this virtually unfathomable number represents not only consumer credit card debt, but mortgages, car loans, and of course habitual overspending for double decaf nonfat lattes. With the proliferation of a debt-based society, one of the fastest growing industries is naturally collection agencies, who help provide employment for individuals who would otherwise be forced to become ax-murders or even more serious felons.

Right now, there are over 17,000 collection agencies across the nation harassing a substantial portion of the American citizenry, and that probably includes you. As a matter of fact, over the past five years, the number of people who have been contacted by debt collectors exceeds the residents of Florida, New Jersey, and The People's Republic of China combined.

However, with the rampant rise of collection agencies has come another cottage industry: so-called consumer credit services. These companies, working in cahoots with the banks to prevent individuals at any cost from declaring bankruptcy, offer to lower interest charges by "consolidating" all your minor debts into one colossal monthly sum, effectively stretching out your monthly payments to the year 3006.

Indeed, when you add up all the bloodsuckers involved in the field of debt collection, including entire divisions of transnational banks, endless multitudes of low rent lawyers, plus several guys named Vinnie from The Bronx, it's enough to make you upchuck.

Fortunately, there is a powerful and compelling answer to the problem of debt. But to achieve true peace of mind, you first need to focus on our your silly anxiety about not paying your credit card bills.

According to a recent survey, the terror of being in debt, being contacted by a collection agency, or simply having one's precious credit rating blemished are among the most pervasive fears facing Americans today, even more terrifying than J. Lo's next movie!

There is an immense resentment against financial institutions who charge consumers in excess of 28% interest on their Visa and Master Cards, often hiking their rates and penalties without prior notice. According to Bankrate.com, card issuers routinely bump up late fees and over-the-limit fees on card debt and shorten payment grace periods. Fee income -- the bulk of which comes from penalty fees -- accounts for more than 30 percent of card-issuers' profits. For many of the credit card top issuers, it has reached 40 percent!

Even more troubling, their monopolistic tactics go virtually unopposed by a Pro-Banking Administration. Paid-off politicians who recently stripped away most consumer protections and instituted a new bankruptcy law, one that will penalize millions of hardworking individuals and give the banks their last pound of flesh.

As a matter of fact, it's surprising they also didn't propose flogging people with credit problems, throwing them into debtor's prisons or forcing them to appear on Jerry Springer. But our suggestion is don't get angry, get even with all these banking industry swine. Get even for their usury credit practices, their deceptive advertising, and of course their debt collectors who without fail lack the basic humanity of Saddam Hussein.

On top of that, adding insult to injury, millions of Americans like yourself are confronted with debts they NEVER even incurred. Thanks to the incredibly lax and inadequate security procedures set up by the banks, all those high tech measures they supposedly insituted to safeguard your identity in the first place.

It seems like only yesterday (as a matter of fact it WAS only yesterday) that 40 million names and credit numbers were stolen by hackers from a single card processing center.

That's 40 MILLION names!

Add this to the millions of other names already stolen and you got a lot of people paying for a lot of stuff that's currently being shipped off to a post office box in Pakistan.

So what's the solution, according to the card companies? Check your statements for any "unauthorized" purchases and then call them, and call them, and CALL them! Waiting your turn patiently to talk to someone in INDIA because there's 39 million other people ahead of you. By the way, why aren't they calling YOU?

That's another story!

Meanwhile, of course, because your credit history has been ruined, identity stolen, home foreclosed, car repossessed, savings seized, you are now so low on the credit totem pole that you don't even qualify for a Discover Card -- the most heinous insult of all!

Here's the bottom line: Do every one of your creditors deserve to driven absolutely and TOTALLY crazy? Don't make us laugh!

CHAPTER FOUR

Observing Cash Wednesday

To get in the mood, here is one small step that you can take right now. A tiny gesture that will penalize all those corporate creditors BIG TIME! The concept is so simple, so easy, it's practically devoid of any effort whatsoever. That's right. There is absolutely nothing for you to do. Even so, it'll make all those folks who issue credit cards want to blow their brains out!

We call it **Cash Wednesday**.

In other words, on Wednesdays, ONLY pay for items in cash. And it doesn't make a difference what you pay cash for: food, gas, CDs, a new stereo, just use good old dollars. Think of it. If everyone in the whole country decided to use cash for only one day, do you know how many billions and billions of dollars in fees and surcharges that would cost the banks?

We guarantee you. It boggles the mind!

Here's the bottom line: They're always hitting you where it hurts -- right in the wallet. So why not return the favor? Hit them back where it hurts -- right in their fat corporate coffers! So take the pledge today. Promise to use only cash on Wednesdays. If all of us act together, we can bring the entire credit card industry to its knees!

Can you imagine, one seventh of their ill-gotten profits disappearing practically overnight. There's no doubt about it. Cash Wednesday is the one national holiday every American should observe all year round!

CHAPTER FIVE

Getting Forward With Creditors

If you prefer not to deal with creditors at all, the phone company has provided a convenient answer for you: Call Forwarding. At those times of the day when creditors call, simply forward their calls to any number you choose.

Can't seem to think of any? Just look through the Yellow Pages. Using a little ingenuity, every day of the week you can forward these bottom feeders to a different number until they tear their hair out.

Here are a few suggestions:

FORWARD YOUR CREDITORS TO:

Funeral Parlors
Proctologists
Transsexual Hotlines
Collection Agencies
Divorce Lawyers
Ex-Mother-In-Laws
Ex-Spouses
Ex-Lovers
Ex-Podiatrists
Their Own Number *(Brilliant Strategy!)*
Insane Asylums
Foreign Embassies
The ASPCA
The CIA
Hollywood Agents
Gay Newspapers
Not-So-Gay Newspapers
The Cleveland Chamber of Commerce

The list goes on and on. Use your imagination and get creative! But please don't forward their calls to 911, hospitals, fire departments, or any other emergency number. That's NOT funny!

CHAPTER SIX

This Approach Really Sounds Funny!

I n the following pages you'll find 30 scenarios. Sample scripts that will give you an idea on how to use the sound effects. As a matter of fact, some of the scripts DON'T even use sound effects. They just give you fun and effective ways for getting rid of these pests. What's more, to keep it simple, the sound effects on the web site (www.funnyguy.com/sfx) or the CD will be numbered the same as in the chapters. So there's no confusion.

Going from chapter to chapter, you'll discover that some scenarios use one sound effect, others two or three. But don't worry. In almost no time, you'll master the techniques like a pro. You'll know exactly when to start the tracks, shut them off, repeat them, or skip forward or backward to another track.

Best of all, you can create many of the sound effects with items you already have around the house: a vacuum cleaner, bathroom plunger, blender, etc. Pretty soon, you'll be modifying sound effects or even creating outrageous new ones to confound creditors.

Let's face it. Being in debt is no fun. But that doesn't mean YOU can't have fun with it! Practice getting into character a few times, or find a sound effect that works for you and improvise a new character. The possibilities are virtually endless.

So forget about all your anxiety. You are safe and secure at home. You are completely in control. That's right. Starting today, your hang-ups about speaking to creditors will be gone forever.

Because you'll be giving THEM all the hang-ups!

Five Steps to Get Started!

1. First place your CD player (or computer) near the phone.

2. Next identify each of your creditors by using Caller ID. If you don't have that feature, just have the CD ready to play the moment you hear their obnoxious voices.

3. Then (after slipping in the disk or clicking your computer sound file) all you have to do is prepare to do a little play-acting on the phone.

4. Replay the same sound effect as many times as you like. Raise and lower the volume for added variety and realism.

5. Then really get creative. Inject new sounds effects and make up even wackier stories! The sky's the limit when dealing with these morons!!

REMEMBER!
All sound effects are available for free download at:
www.funnyguy.com/sfx

Or if you prefer, you may purchase
the SOUND EFFECTS CD at:
www.funnyguy.com/shop.htm

CHAPTER SEVEN

The Ultimate Farting Fiasco

MR. DICK CALLS FRED

FRED: *Hello?*

DICK: *Have I reached the Perdue residence?*

FRED: *You have.*

DICK: *Is this Fred Perdue?*

SFX: **SEVERAL LOUD FARTS**

FRED: *Whoa! Excuse me. Yes, it is.*

DICK: *This is Mr . Dick. Your account has been referred to us for failure to meet your financial obligations.*

FRED: *Well, I lost my job six months ago.*

DICK: *That's tough. Got any savings?*

SFX: **SEVERAL LOUDER FARTS**

FRED: *I'm afraid all my funds have been exhausted.*

DICK: *Are you saying that you have no money to pay this debt now?*

FRED: *Exactly. Because of my internal condition.*

DICK: *Well, we do offer a flexible payment schedule that --*

SFX: **ONE REALLY BIG FART**

FRED: *Oh boy -- Whew! That was a REAL stinkeroo! What has gotten into me!? I just took two bottles of Pepto-Bismol.*

DICK: *As I was saying, we offer a flexible --*

FRED: *Yeah, that could work, as soon as I get another job.*

DICK: *And sir, what are your prospects for that?*

FRED: *Pretty good. As soon as the state of California...*

DICK: *The state of California?*

SFX: **A WHOLE BUNCH OF UNBELIEVABLE FARTS!**

FRED: *...says that I'm no longer an environmental hazard.*

(CLICK!)

CHAPTER EIGHT

The Dentist's Drill Delusion

MR. DICK CALLS JERRY

JERRY: Hello.

DICK: Stay on the line. Do not hang up. Hanging up is not an option.

JERRY: Fine with me.

DICK: You may not hang up under any circumstances.

JERRY: I told you, I'm not going anywhere.

DICK: Jerry Alexander?

JERRY: The one and only.

DICK: I'm Mr. Dick. And I am.... And I am required to inform you that this call may be recorded for quality control.

JERRY: That's a very good idea.

DICK: *The purpose of this call is to determine why you have failed to respond to our previous attempts to contact you.*

SFX: **DENTIST'S DRILL**

JERRY: *Awwwwrgh! Argggghhhh!*

DICK: *Mr. Alexander?*

JERRY: *Please go on.*

DICK: *Are you at the dentist's office?*

JERRY: *No, I have my own drill.*

DICK: *Your own drill?*

JERRY: *It's cheaper. Besides, it's not like I can charge this filling to my credit card, is it?*

DICK: *I suppose not.*

JERRY: *Unless you increase my limit by another five hundred dollars.*

DICK: *That's not going to happen. Mr. Alexander, we really have to know when --*

SFX: **DRILLING**

JERRY: *Arrrrfffffgggggghhhhhh!! Argggghowawawahhh!! Whoa, almost... have all the decay out.*

DICK: *Don't you think you should at least use anesthesia?*

JERRY: *Who's got money for anesthesia?*

DICK: *Be that as it may, when can we expect a payment?*

JERRY: *What incredible nerve you have!*

DICK: *Were you talking to me?*

JERRY: *No, to me. I was looking at my tooth in the mirror.*

SFX: **DRILLING**

JERRY: *ARRRRRGGGGGHHHH!!! ARRRRRGHHHH!!!!! OWWWWWWHHHHHH! Man. That doesn't look good. That doesn't look good at all. That damn molar is going to need root canal work.*

DICK: *Perhaps I should call back at a better time.*

JERRY: *Okay. Now where did I put that corkscrew?*

(CLICK!)

CHAPTER NINE

The Insane Asylum Scheme

MR. DICK CALLS VICTOR

SFX:	**NUT HOUSE!**
VICTOR:	*Hello. Ward Six*
DICK:	*I have an urgent call for Victor Moscowitz.*
VICTOR:	*Is this his therapist?*
DICK:	*No, this is Mr. Dick. And I must speak to him without delay.*
VICTOR :	*I see. Do you know his diagnosis?*
DICK:	*What do you mean?*
VICTOR :	*Well, we have patients divided by their mental condition.*
DICK:	*I'm just looking for Victor Moscowitz. Is he around?*
VICTOR:	*Sir, I'm trying to help you. Is the patient's name Victor Moscowitz, or is that just one of his delusions?*

DICK: *What are you talking about?*

VICTOR: *Many of our patients suffer from delusions. There's one woman here who thinks she's Napoleon's podiatrist.*

DICK: *That's fascinating. This is the number Victor Moscowitz put on his credit application.*

VICTOR: *Then he must be crazy.*

DICK: *Crazy or not, I want to speak to him.*

VICTOR: *You want to speak to a crazy person?*

DICK: *Yes I do.*

VICTOR: *That's insane. Perhaps you should drop by.*

DICK: *Okay, let's regroup here. Victor Moscowitz is 37 years old. Do you have anyone there who is 37 years old?*

VICTOR: *We have one ward where everyone claims to be 37 years old.*

DICK: *That's nuts!*

VICTOR: *Exactly. Perhaps you can be more specific. Is he schizophrenic? Manic-Depressive? Paranoid?*

DICK: *Probably Paranoid.*

VICTOR: *Great. Now we're getting somewhere. Is it a persecution complex stemming from childhood factors? Is it an obsession associated with a traumatic experience? Is it a deep suspicion of foreigners. Is it --*

DICK: *What about a fear of collection agencies?*

VICTOR: *Collecto-Phobia! Why didn't you say so in the first place?*

DICK: *I thought I did. Do you have anyone there with Collecto-Phobia?*

VICTOR: *Sorry, not a soul.*

(CLICK!)

CHAPTER TEN

The Morris Studio Maneuver

Remember, if you see that a creditor is calling, you're under no obligation to identify yourself. So simply pretend your number is a fictitious place of business, an office or studio or whatever you choose. Then you can instantly switch the tables on whatever moron is on the line. Plus for this approach, you DON'T even need sound effects!

MR. DICK CALLS HECTOR

HECTOR: *Good Morning. Morris Studios.*

DICK: *Please put Hector Witherspoon on the phone.*

HECTOR: *Who's calling, please?*

DICK: *Mr. Dick.*

HECTOR: *Dick, what studio is he in?*

DICK: *What do you mean, what studio is he in?*

HECTOR: *Well, he would have to be in one of our studios. We have seventeen studios and they're all occupied at the moment.*

DICK: *What kind of place is this?*

HECTOR: *Are you sure you have the right number?*

DICK: *I'm absolutely sure. This is the number Hector Witherspoon gave us.*

HECTOR: *When?*

DICK: *I don't know when. This is the number we have for him.*

HECTOR: *Well, this is the general studio number.*

DICK: *For what?*

HECTOR: *Morris Studios.*

DICK: *What's Morris Studios?*

HECTOR: *Didn't the person you're trying to reach tell you?*

DICK: *No, he didn't.*

HECTOR: *Then I'm not permitted to give that information out. Perhaps you should call Hector at home and leave him a message.*

DICK: *This is his home number.*

HECTOR: *No, this is the home of Morris Studios.*

DICK: *Alright, alright. Could you do me a favor?*

HECTOR: *Sure.*

DICK: *Could you go around to the studios and see if Hector Witherspoon is in any of them.*

HECTOR: *You mean knock on all the doors?*

DICK: *Uh-huh.*

HECTOR: *And ask if he's inside?*

DICK: *Exactly.*

HECTOR: *That's out of the question. What happens inside the studios is strictly confidential.*

DICK: *Why's that?*

HECTOR: *If I told you, it wouldn't be confidential.*

DICK: *Here's what. If Hector Witherspoon just happens to pass by --*

HECTOR: *How would I know if he passed by? What does he look like?*

DICK: *I don't know what he looks like!*

HECTOR: *You're making it very difficult for me to help you.*

DICK: *Look, isn't there someone else I can speak to?*

HECTOR: *Of course. But right now, they're all in the studios.*

DICK: *In that case, just put me through to any studio.*

HECTOR: *Which studio would you like?*

DICK: *I don't know. I don't know. Studio eleven.*

HECTOR: *Who do you wish to speak to in Studio Eleven?*

DICK: *How the hell would I know!?*

HECTOR: *I'm sorry. You'll have to be more specific.*

(CLICK!)

CHAPTER ELEVEN

The Vacuum Cleaner Vendetta

MR. DICK CALLS EDNA

EDNA: *Hello.*

DICK: *Edna Willoughby?*

EDNA: *Yes. Who's this?*

DICK: *Mr. Dick. Your account has been referred to us for immediate collection. This call may be recorded for training and quality control purposes.*

SFX: **VACUUM CLEANER.
LOW SETTING.**

EDNA: *Could you please speak up?*

DICK: *I said this call may be recorded.*

EDNA: *Fine with me.*

DICK: *Miss Willoughby. You have exhausted the patience of this institution. We have offered to work with you, but it seems you have zero interest in resolving this matter.*

EDNA: *Got ya!*

DICK: *Are you speaking to me?*

EDNA: *No. To that dust ball I was after.*

DICK: *Would it be possible to turn off the vacuum while we're talking?*

EDNA: *Turn it off? I never turn it off! Those scummy dust balls are everywhere. All over the place! But they can't hide from me!*

SFX: **VACUUM CLEANER.**
MEDIUM SETTING.

DICK: *Miss Willoughby? Miss Willoughby!?*

EDNA: *Could you please speak up?*

DICK: *Miss Willoughby, when can we expect some positive action on your part?*

EDNA: *Where are you? Come out of there! Oh I see you alright! Trying to hide under the couch? I'm gonna suck you up right now! Got ya -- ya filthy bugger! Right in the bag!*

DICK: *Miss Willoughby, I'm thrilled you like to keep a clean house. But how about cleaning up your account with us. It's still not too late. If you make a payment today, I can work out a monthly schedule to fit your budget.*

EDNA: *Sorry, all my money goes to Hoover and Eureka.*

DICK: *Your children?*

EDNA: *My vacuum cleaners! I've got a whole army of dust busters at my disposal. I have uprights and handhelds. Rotating Brushes. Dirt Indicators. Cyclonic suction!*

DICK: *Miss Willoughby, can't we discuss this matter like --*

EDNA: *Come here, my little Oreck, we have work to do!*

SFX: **VACUUM CLEANER.
HIGH SETTING.**

DICK: *Miss Willoughby? Miss Willoughby!*

EDNA: *Come out, come out, wherever you are! Now I got you trapped. Thought you could sneak under the fridge, huh? Ha-Ha-Ha! Got ya! And your little dust buddies too!!*

DICK: *MISS WILLOUGHBY!! CAN YOU TURN THAT VACUUM CLEANER OFF FOR ONE MINUTE!!!? JUST FOR ONE GODDAMN LOUSY STINKIN' MINUTE!!! YOU ARE OUT OF CONTROL!! YOU NEED PROFESSIONAL HELP! DO YOU HEAR ME, MISS WILLOUGHBY!? DO YOU UNDERSTAND WHAT I'M SAYING!!!?*

EDNA: *By the way, do you know a good carpet cleaner?*

(CLICK!)

REMEMBER!
All sound effects are available for free download at:
www.funnyguy.com/sfx

Or if you prefer, you may purchase
the SOUND EFFECTS CD at:
www.funnyguy.com/shop.htm

CHAPTER TWELVE

The Colonic Counter Attack

MR. DICK CALLS TERRY

TERRY: *Hi!*

DICK: *Can you please put Terry on the line.*

TERRY: *Terry Who?*

DICK: *Terry McCall*

TERRY: *You got her.*

DICK: *This is Mr. Dick and I've been instructed to contact you about a personal debt.*

TERRY: *To society?*

DICK: *No, to the Cleveland International Bank.*

SFX: **TOILET FLUSHING**

TERRY: *Please go on.*

DICK: *Uh, the bank has a very firm policy on people who miss their payments.*

TERRY: *How firm would you say? On a scale of one to ten.*

DICK: *Look, it's very firm.*

SFX: **TOILET FLUSHING**

TERRY: *Please go on.*

DICK: *There are serious penalties involved.*

TERRY: *Really. How serious? On a scale of one to ten.*

SFX: **TOILET FLUSHING**

DICK: *Ten, okay! Do you have to keep on flushing that toilet!?*

TERRY: *Oh, I'm sorry. Does it disturb you.*

DICK: *Yes, very much.*

TERRY: *Okay, I'll try to stop.*

DICK: *Thank you.*

TERRY: *Although it's hard. I just gave myself a colonic. You know, in order to maintain optimum health, you have to give yourself at least seven colonics every day.*

DICK: *Whatever works for you. When will you be able to --*

SFX: **TOILET FLUSHING**

TERRY: *Please go on. I didn't hear you.*

DICK: *DO YOU HAVE TO KEEP ON FLUSHING THAT TOILET!?*

TERRY: *Oh no, no. Not anymore. All done. Finished.*

DICK: *Thank God!*

TERRY: *All cleaned out. All blockages removed. All toxins eliminated.*

DICK: *I'm thrilled for you. Can we return to --*

SFX: **TOILET FLUSHING**

TERRY: *Wow! Where did that one come from? Out of the clear blue. I swear you never know when they're going to hit you. Now, what were you saying?*

DICK: *Terry, the Cleveland International Bank would very much like you to meet the fiscal obligation that you --*

SFX: **FEET SLOSHING THROUGH WATER**

TERRY: *Please go on. I'm looking for my plunger. Everything is overflowing here. Where is that lousy thing? I just had it. Oh yuck, there goes my pedicure...*

(CLICK!)

CHAPTER THIRTEEN

The Stranger In Paradise Plan

MR. DICK CALLS WILBUR

SFX: **OCEAN WAVES, UKELELES, & NATIVES**

WILBUR: *Hello, whoever you are.*

DICK: *This is Mr. Dick.*

WILBUR: *Hello Mr. Dick, hello, hello, hello, whoever you are.*

DICK: *Have you been drinking?*

WILBUR: *Yes, coconut milk and native rum. Ahhhh....
Hits the spot!*

DICK: *Wilbur Griffin, I recognize your voice.*

WILBUR: *I applaud your memory. I applaud each one of the grey
cells in your tiny little brain.*

DICK: *Being abusive is not going to help your situation.*

WILBUR: *It's not going to hurt it, either.*

DICK: *Wilbur, this is my last phone call to you.*

WILBUR: *Promises, promises.*

DICK: *The patience of my bank has just about reached an end. We issued you not one, not two, but three credit cards. You had a superb credit record for eighteen years. Not one missed payment, not one late payment, not one time did you stray over your limit.*

WILBUR: *I was a pillar of the credit community.*

DICK: *Indeed you were. And now where are you?*

WILBUR: *To tell you the truth, I'm not really sure.*

DICK: *From the sound of it, you're either down in Florida or out in Hawaii. But sooner or later, my friend, you'll have to return to Beaumont Drive.*

WILBUR: *You're absolutely right. There's no way to avoid facing my financial responsibilities…*

DICK: *I'm glad you see my point.*

WILBUR: *In about twenty years.*

DICK: *What are you talking about?*

WILBUR: *I'm talking about outsourcing.*

DICK: *I'm not following.*

WILBUR: *Five months ago, my job was outsourced to one of those third world countries. You know, one of those tropical countries over in Asia. One of those places where they pay people about fifteen cents an hour.*

DICK: *I'm very sympathetic. But you've maxed out your cards and your outstanding balance is now almost thirty-five thousand dollars.*

WILBUR: *Thirty-five thousand? That's nothing!*

DICK: *That's nothing?*

WILBUR: *In America. But here where I am, it's a fortune.*

DICK: *And just where are you?*

WILBUR: *Oh, you might say I just followed my job across the sea. Like a little seagull, I flapped my wings and here I am in paradise.*

DICK: *Let me get this straight. You're in some foreign country. The same foreign country where your job went?*

WILBUR: *You are so perceptive.*

DICK: *And you're living off your credit cards?*

WILBUR: *Not just living. LIVING!*

DICK: *Wilbur, you may have your little fantasy life now, but the reality is we're going to find you.*

WILBUR: *Well, bring a lot of suntan lotion. You're going to need it.*

DICK: You can't hide forever.

WILBUR: A quaint notion. I used to think that way. Anyhow, I've got to go.

DICK: We're not through yet.

WILBUR: I hate to be rude. But it's time for my three 'o' clock massage.

DICK: Wilbur!

WILBUR: Then it will be time for my four 'o' clock massage.

DICK: Wilbur!!

WILBUR: Followed by my five 'o' clock massage.
My six 'o' clock mas—

(CLICK!)

WILBUR: Whoops, my mistake, at six I have my body scrub…

CHAPTER FOURTEEN

The Cat Food Fake-Out

MR. DICK CALLS ETHAN

ETHAN: *This is Ethan.*

DICK: *Ethan Mellanger?*

ETHAN: *Speaking.*

DICK: *Mr. Mellanger.*

ETHAN: *Please call me Ethan.*

DICK: *Ethan, I'm Mr. Dick. I've been trying to reach you for two weeks.*

ETHAN: *I know. I heard the phone ringing.*

DICK: *Then why didn't you answer?*

ETHAN: *I was too weak.*

DICK: *Too weak?*

ETHAN: *From hunger. I ran out of food three weeks ago.*

SFX: **CAT MEOWING**

DICK: *Uh, I'm sorry to hear that.*

ETHAN: *Things are so bad I've had to eat cat food for the past six months.*

DICK: *That's tough. But even so, you realize you have an obligation to repay the loan our company made to you.*

ETHAN: *And I have every intention of doing that, as soon as I get something to eat.*

SFX: **CAT MEOWING LOUDER**

DICK: *Is your cat hungry too?*

ETHAN: *Oh, that's not my cat. She belongs to the gay couple downstairs.*

DICK: *I see. Mr. Mellanger.*

ETHAN: *Call me Ethan.*

DICK: *Ethan, when do you think you'll be able to raise some funds?*

ETHAN: *As soon as I start working.*

DICK: *And when will that be?*

ETHAN: *As soon as I have the strength to work.*

SFX: **CAT CRIES!**

DICK: *Is everything all right?*

ETHAN: *Perfectly. I'm just getting some cat food.*

DICK: *Down at the store?*

ETHAN: *No. I make it at home. Freshly made cat food.*

SFX: **BLENDER.**
CAT SOUNDS TERRIFIED!

DICK: *Mr. Mellanger? Mr. Mellanger?*

ETHAN: *Be right with you. Come here little kitty. Don't be afraid.*

DICK: *Mr. Mellanger!?*

ETHAN: *Got ya! Oh, scratch me, you little SOB!! Take that!*

SFX: **BLENDER ON HIGH.**
CAT WAILS!

SILENCE.

DICK: *Mr. Mellanger?*

ETHAN: *Aaaaaah. I love Persians. Hits the spot every time!*
You were saying?

(CLICK!)

CHAPTER FIFTEEN

The CIA Paranoia Proviso

MR. DICK CALLS SUZANNE

SUZANNE: *Hello.*

DICK: *By federal law, I have to confirm your identity.*

SUZANNE: *Well, first I have to confirm yours.*

DICK: *What do you mean you have to confirm mine?*

SUZANNE: *Well, I'm not going to confirm my identity to anyone whose identity isn't confirmed.*

DICK: *Listen lady, I have to confirm that I'm speaking to Suzanne Klopman.*

SUZANNE: *I'll confirm I'm Suzanne Klopman when you confirm you're NOT Stanley Hotchkiss from the CIA.*

DICK: *What are you talking about?*

SFX: **HIGH TECH ELECTRONIC NOISES**

SUZANNE: *Hear that. I've switched on my Automatic Identity Detector.*

DICK: *Your what?*

SUZANNE: *By the stress level in your voice, it will tell me whether you're being truthful or not.*

DICK: *This is crazy!*

SUZANNE: *This is science. Are you or are you not Stanley Hotchkiss from the CIA?*

DICK: *Okay, okay, I'm not Stanley Hotchkiss from the CIA.*

SUZANNE: *But are you confirming you're not Stanley Hotchkiss?*

DICK: *Yes, yes, of course I'm confirming that --*

SFX: **HIGH TECH BUZZING NOISES**

SUZANNE: *Inconclusive. Your response is insufficiently valid. I'll have to further confirm you're not Stanley Hotchkiss from the CIA.*

DICK: *This is unbelievable. I have a very important matter to--*

SUZANNE: *So your wife's name is not Louise Hotchkiss?*

DICK: *We have a claim that has to be --*

SUZANNE: *Just confirm that your wife's name it not Louise Hotchkiss. What are you hiding?*

DICK: *I'm not hiding anything. There is an outstanding balance of --*

SFX: **HIGH TECH WARNING NOISES**

SUZANNE: *Evasive reaction. You're not helping your case any.*

DICK: *My case? I'm calling about your case.*

SUZANNE: *Irrelevant answer.*

DICK: *Irrelevant? What in the world are you --*

SUZANNE: *Confirm you don't live at 317 Perlmutter Drive.*

VINCENT: *I don't even know where Perlmutter Drive is!*

SFX: **HIGH TECH HUMMING NOISES**

SUZANNE: *That's been verified.*

DICK: *That's just great. What else do you want to know!?*

SUZANNE: *One last thing. Confirm your brother-in-law isn't Morris Schwartz.*

DICK: *I'M NOT EVEN MARRIED!*

SFX: **HIGH TECH POPS AND WHISTLES**

SUZANNE: *Confirmed. I now feel safe in assuming you're not Stanley Hotchkiss from the CIA.*

DICK: *That's right. That's absolutely right! I'm not Stanley Hotchkiss. Do you hear me? I'm not Stanley Hotchkiss from the CIA! I'm Mr. Dick!! MR. DICK from Federal Savings!!!*

SUZANNE: *Can you confirm that?*

(CLICK!)

CHAPTER SIXTEEN

The Double Espresso Manifesto

MR. DICK CALLS ROBERT

SFX: **CROWDED COFFEE SHOP**

ROBERT: *(JITTERY) Who-who-who is it?*

DICK: *Is this Mr. Robert Clements?*

ROBERT: *(TALKING REAL FAST) Yes yes yes yes yes yes indeed!*

DICK: *This is Mr. Dick. We have to --*

ROBERT: *Wait wait wait wait wait -- I have to get my coffee!*

DICK: *Can we --*

ROBERT: *My scrumptuous umptuous triple grand mocha espresso cappuchino frappachino!*

DICK: *You have an outstanding...*

ROBERT: *Yesssssssssssireeeeeeeee! Whoa! Gotta have that Caffeine BLAST!!! YA-HOOOOOOOO! WHAT A RUSH!!!*

DICK: *Balance of over three thousand and --*

ROBERT: *Whawhatwhawhawhawha YOU SAY!? --
I need a cup of coffee!*

DICK: *You just had a cup of--*

ROBERT: *EEEEEEEEEEEEEEEHHHHH--THEY'RE ALL OUT OF FRENCH ROASTED COFFEE BEANS!!!*

DICK: *Look we need payment by --*

ROBERT: *Sorrysorrysorrysorrysorrysorrysorry...*

DICK: *The 17th or your account will be --*

ROBERT: *OOOOOOOOOOOOHHH!
Gottagottagottagogottagogottago-gottagogottago...*

DICK: *To the bathroom?*

ROBERT: *No, to Starbucks!*

(CLICK!)

CHAPTER SEVENTEEN

The Emergency Room Scenario

MR. DICK CALLS OLGA

SFX: **HEART MONITOR BEEPING**

OLGA: *(LOW, WEAK VOICE) Yes.*

DICK: *Is this Olga Willowbanks?*

OLGA: *Yes.*

DICK: *This is Mr. Dick and I'm calling about an extremely urgent business matter.*

OLGA: *Yes.*

DICK: *Our records indicate your account is seriously overdue and --*

SFX: **FASTER BEEPING**

DICK: *What's that?*

OLGA: *It's nothing.*

DICK: *Sounds like you're in the Emergency Room?*

OLGA: *There's nothing wrong with me! I'm fine! I'm fine! I don't care what the doctors say!!*

SFX: **EVEN FASTER BEEPING!**

DICK: *Okay, okay, relax, settle down, okay...*

OLGA: *Okay.*

DICK: *Take a deep breath or something.*

OLGA: *Okay.*

SFX: **NORMAL BEEPING AGAIN**

DICK: *Maybe I should call back at a better time.*

OLGA: *No really, I'm okay. It's nothing. What can I do for you?*

DICK: *You sure?*

OLGA: *Yes, I'm sure.*

DICK: *Well, according to our records, because you've exceeded your credit limit by 400 dollars, we going to have to cancel your --*

SFX: **SCARY FLAT-LINING SOUND!**

OLGA: *Urrrrgggghhhhh....*

DICK: *Miss Willowbanks?*

OLGA: *URRRRRGGGGGHHHH...*

DICK: *Miss Willowbanks!? MISS WILLOWBANKS!!?*

OLGA: *Once again, you'll have to cancel what?*

(CLICK!)

CHAPTER EIGHTEEN

The Sexual Encounter Subterfuge

MR. DICK CALLS DAVID

DAVID: *(Out of Breath) Hello.*

DICK: *Am I speaking to David Kabosch?*

DAVID: *Yes, you are.*

DICK: *This is Mr. Dick. Did I catch you in the middle of something?*

DAVID: *No, not really.*

DICK: *Okay, the reason I'm calling is about your last gold card payment.*

SFX: **WOMAN'S VOICE -- Oh yes...yes!**

DICK: *Excuse me, is there someone else there?*

DAVID: *Where?*

DICK: *With you.*

DAVID: *Oh, just my girlfriend. But I can multi-task.*

DICK: *Look, I can call back later.*

DAVID: *No, this is a good time to talk. Really. You've got my complete attention.*

SFX: **WOMAN'S VOICE -- Oh my God...yeah... right over...**

DICK: *What were we, uh ---*

DAVID: *My last gold card payment.*

DICK: *Yes, that's right. It's five months overdue.*

DAVID: *Five months, you say?*

DICK: *Five months.*

SFX: **WOMAN'S VOICE -- Don't stop...I'm almost there....Oh...!**

DAVID: *That is way overdue. Let me check my records.*

DICK: *Your records?*

DAVID: *Don't worry. I have a headset. It frees up my hands for other things.*

SFX: **WOMAN'S VOICE -- Baby, Baby, Oh, Oh, Baby!**

DICK: *Maybe this is not the --*

DAVID: *Let's see. Where is that last bank statement? Hold on, I'm looking for it.*

DICK: *Okay, I'll wait.*

DAVID: *Now where did I put that thing? It's not under the pillow. Hmmm. It's not under the blanket. Boy, it's not even under the sheets.*

DICK: *Really, we can do this another --*

SFX: **WOMAN'S VOICE -- ORGASMIC -- Yes! Yes!!! Oh!! Oh!!!!!**

DAVID: *Found it! You'll never guess where it was. Feels a trifle damp, though.*

(CLICK!)

REMEMBER!

All sound effects are available for free download at:

www.funnyguy.com/sfx

Or if you prefer, you may purchase
the SOUND EFFECTS CD at:

www.funnyguy.com/shop.htm

CHAPTER NINETEEN

The Homeless Proposition

MR. DICK CALLS MATTHEW

MATTHEW:	*Hello.*
COMPUTER VOICE:	*This is the law office of Godfrey and Schmidt. Please hold the line for a representative.*
MATTHEW:	*Hello? Hello?*
COMPUTER VOICE:	*A representative will be with you shortly. Do NOT hang up!*
MATTHEW:	*Okay.*
DICK:	*This is Mr. Dick. To whom am I speaking?*

MATTHEW:	Mathew. Mathew Shear.
DICK:	Mr. Shear, your account has been referred to us for collection. Do you have any intent to pay the amount you owe?
SFX:	**LOCOMOTIVE & NEARBY TRAIN WHISTLE**
MATTHEW:	*Well, uh...*
DICK:	*Speak up. I can't hear you.*
SFX:	**LOCOMOTIVE GETTING LOUDER**
MATTHEW:	*As soon as this train passes...*
DICK:	*What? What train?*
MATTHEW:	*Well, ever since they took my house, I've been living down by the train tracks.*
DICK:	*What's your present address?*
MATTHEW:	*Let's see. I'm near the railroad crossing on Main Street, third furniture box down from Bed, Bath & Beyond.*
DICK:	*Are you saying you're homeless?*
SFX:	**LOUD TRAIN WHISTLE**
MATTHEW:	*Whew! That was a close one! Could you run that by me again?*
DICK:	*Look Shear, if you're hiding any assets, we're going to find them.*

MATTHEW: *You mean like my car?*

DICK: *Yeah, just like your car. I guarantee we'll get that too!*

SFX: **RAILROAD TRAIN HITTING CAR.**
    KA-BOOM!!

MATTHEW: *Oh man, there goes the BMW. No insurance*
    either, damn!

(CLICK!)

CHAPTER TWENTY

The Dead Dog Conspiracy

MR. DICK CALLS HERBIE

HERBIE: *Hello.*

DICK: *Herbie Milksap?*

HERBIE: *The same.*

DICK: *This is Mr. Dick. I've been leaving messages for you for over six weeks. Why haven't you returned my calls?*

HERBIE: *Haven't I? Hmmm...*

SFX: **DOGS HOWLING MOURNFULLY**

DICK: *What's that?*

HERBIE: *What's what?*

DICK: *It sounds like you're in a kennel.*

HERBIE: *I beg your pardon. Those are all the mourners who've come over to pay their respects to FiFi.*

DICK: *Your wife?*

HERBIE: *My darling little Chihuahua. She was so young --*

SFX: **SINGLE DOG WAILING OUT LOUD**

HERBIE: *Oh Toodles. Try to be strong! Someday you'll see your Fifi again.*

DICK: *I know this is a bad time to call, but you're totally maxed out.*

HERBIE: *Well, all those specialists and trips to the doggie spa were expensive. But nothing was too good for my little Fifi. Nothing!*

SFX: **BARKING LOUDLY IN AGREEMENT**

DICK: *Mr. Milksap, all I want to know is when you are going to make a payment. Can you commit to a definite date?*

HERBIE: *To tell you the truth, I've gotten an attorney to represent me.*

DICK: *In that case, give me your attorney's name and I won't be bothering you any more.*

HERBIE: *You're in luck. My attorney just happens to be here. Maybe you guys can reach a settlement. Say hello to Maxie...*

DICK: *Hello Maxie. How are you?*

SFX: **DOBERMAN GROWLING**

DICK: *Maxie? You son-of-a--*

(CLICK!)

REMEMBER!
All sound effects are available for free download at:
www.funnyguy.com/sfx

Or if you prefer, you may purchase
the SOUND EFFECTS CD at:
www.funnyguy.com/shop.htm

CHAPTER TWENTY-ONE

The Buy-Sexual Strategy

MR. DICK CALLS MINDY

SFX: **DEPARTMENT STORE**

DICK: *Please stay on the line. This is not a sales call.*

MINDY: *Too bad.*

DICK: *Too bad?*

MINDY: *Yes, I LOVE sales calls. Because I love to buy buy buy! Buying is my life. As a matter of fact, I'm down at the mall right now. I'm ALWAYS down at the mall. Got to keep the economy going. You're sure this isn't a sales call?*

DICK: *This is about a late payment. You haven't made a payment in six months. Unless you pay your entire balance today, your account will be turned over to our collections department.*

MINDY: *What are they selling?*

DICK: *They're not selling anything.*

MINDY: *Well, if they're not selling anything, I'm not buying.*

DICK: *I don't think you understand.*

MINDY: *I don't think YOU understand. I'm BUY-Sexual.*

DICK: *Look your personal life is your --*

MINDY: *I mean BUY-Sexual. B. U. Y. I simply can't control myself. Every time I walk into Bloomingdales I get multiple STORE-GASMS. I even watch the Home Shopping Network with a vibrator. Why the last time I bought retail I had go to church and say one hundred Hail Macy's!*

DICK: *Lady, I don't want to listen --*

MINDY: *Hey listen, wanna hear about the time I visited The Great MALL of China?*

DICK: *Look lady, I'm just calling about your BALANCE!*

MINDY: *Ooooh... You sound so strong, so macho. Can I pick you up something at VICTORIO'S Secret?*

(CLICK!)

CHAPTER TWENTY-TWO

The Multiple Personality Ploy

E ver feel like you're not yourself? Well now, you can turn that to your advantage! This is a great technique not only for dealing with creditors, but for obnoxious sales people or anyone else you want to give a migraine. Consider it group therapy without the group. NO SOUND EFFECTS NEEDED!

MR. DICK CALLS DAVID

DAVID: *Hello. Press one if you want to speak to David. Two if you want Philip. Three if you want Benny. Four if you want Michelle. Five if you want Puffy. Six if you want Richard. Seven if you want Raul. Eight if you want Marilyn. Nine to schedule a conference call. And zero to repeat this menu.*

DICK: *Uh, Uh... (HE PRESSES ONE)*

DAVID: *Hello.*

DICK: *Is this David?*

DAVID: *No, this is Benny.*

DICK: *I pressed one. I thought that was David's line.*

DAVID: *It is.*

DICK: *In that case, could I speak to him?*

DAVID: *You are speaking to him, in a manner of speaking.*

DICK: *I'm not following.*

DAVID: *What's there to follow?*

DICK: *Am I speaking to David or am I not?*

DAVID: *Yes you are, and yes you're not.*

DICK: *Listen, I'm calling about an extremely urgent business matter and it's absolutely necessary that I speak to David right now.*

DAVID: *I'll see if he's here.*

DICK: *Thank you.*

DAVID: *Well, he's here but he's not. Perhaps you'd like to speak to Richard or Michelle.*

DICK: *I don't want Richard or Michelle. I want David.*

DAVID: *Well, Richard and Michelle are closer to David than I am. David doesn't even know that I exist.*

DICK: *Benny, this is too much for me.*

DAVID: *You? What about me? You think it's easy living like this? Not once has David ever acknowledged me. Even to his therapist.*

DICK: *How would you know what he says to his therapist?*

DAVID: *Because I'm there in every session.*

DICK: *You mean, he drags you along?*

DAVID: *Yeah, he drags me and Raul and Puffy and Marilyn and the rest of us and frankly, we're not too thrilled about it.*

DICK: *So let me get this straight. You're all in group therapy?*

DAVID: *We're in Group Personality Therapy. And I for one, am sick of it!*

DICK: *Why's that?*

DAVID: *David is so irresponsible. He spends and spends and racks up these huge credit card debts and there's nothing I can do about it. I try to tell him to be more responsible, to pay his bills, but he never even once hears me.*

DICK: *He ignores you?*

DAVID: *Worse than ignores me. He listens to all the other voices in his head, but not me. Not me! It's like I don't even exist, which frankly I don't.*

DAVID: *Uh Benny, will David be back anytime soon?*

DICK: *David should be returning any minute. Then again, he could be back in an hour, a week, a year, who the hell knows? He doesn't tell me. He doesn't tell anybody. Out of the blue, he just shows up. Not any consideration whatsoever for his other personalities.*

DAVID: *Uh, I'll get back to you.*

DICK: *It probably won't be me.*

(CLICK!)

CHAPTER TWENTY-THREE

The Forgiving Faith Fantasy

MR. DICK CALLS BRETT

BRETT: *Hello.*

DICK: *This is not a solicitation.*

BRETT: *What's a solicitation?*

DICK: *I mean, I'm not trying to sell you anything.*

BRETT: *Then why are you calling?*

DICK: *I'm calling for the purposes of collecting a debt.*

SFX: **WEIRD CHANTING**

BRETT: *Could you speak a little louder. The ceremony has just started.*

DICK: *Ceremony? Where are you?*

BRETT: *In temple. I had my calls forwarded to my cell phone.*

DICK: *Okay, in that case, I'll make it brief. You have an outstanding balance on your account of --*

SFX: **CHANTING GETS MORE INTENSE.**

BRETT: *Could you speak a little louder?*

DICK: *On your account, you have a balance of $3657.48.*

BRETT: *$3657.48?*

DICK: *Exactly.*

BRETT: *Well, I've been forgiven that.*

DICK: *What are you talking about?*

BRETT: *My religion. My faith.*

DICK: *I'm not following.*

BRETT: *My religion forgives all sins -- and all debts. Therefore, I don't owe you anything.*

SFX: **CHANTING GETS MORE FRANTIC**

DICK: *Your religion can't forgive your debts. Only we can forgive your debts. And we're not forgiving you one cent!*

BRETT: *Well, I forgive you for that.*

DICK: *I don't care if you forgive me or not! When are you going to pay us the balance of $3657.48!?*

BRETT: *Perhaps, in my next lifetime.*

SFX: **GONG!**

DICK: *Brett? Brett!?*

BRETT: *(Chanting) Nam Yo Ho Visa Renge Master Card Hare American Krishna Express Hallelujah Discover Om Om Om...*

(CLICK!)

CHAPTER TWENTY-FOUR

The Ominous Suicidal Situation

DICK CALLS MARTY

MARTY: *Hello. This is Marty.*

DICK: *Marty Zimler?*

MARTY: *I'm afraid so.*

DICK: *Marty, this is Mr. Dick. I'm an attorney with Schmidt, Schmidt, Schmidt, & Dick.*

MARTY: *I see. You're probably calling about my credit card debt.*

DICK: *That's correct. Right now, there is serious damage being done to your credit score.*

MARTY: *You mean, negative reports and all that?*

DICK: *It's not a good situation. But there's still hope.*

SFX: **PILLS BEING SPILLED OUT**

MARTY: *Hope? I used to hope there was hope. Day and night I would hope. Hope to find some hope. Not a lot of hope, just a little hope. A teeny weeny bit of hope.*

SFX: **GLASS OF WATER BEING POURED**

DICK: *Are you taking vitamins or something?*

MARTY: *Well, anyone who takes vitamins has hope. Hope that one day things will be better. Can vitamin C or E or D guarantee that? I don't think so.*

DICK: *Look Marty, what are we going to do fix this problem?*

MARTY: *To fix a problem, you must have hope the problem can be fixed. Do you see what I'm saying?*

DICK: *Not really.*

MARTY: *Excuse me.*

SFX: **GULPING DOWN WATER AND PILLS**

DICK: *What are you taking? Aspirin or something?*

MARTY: *Something much better than Aspirin. Something that will take away all my headaches.*

DICK: *Excedrin?*

MARTY: *Something that will take away all my pain and suffering forever. All my anxiety, all my tension, all my feelings of failure and inadequacy...*

DICK: *Valium? Prozac?*

MARTY: *(GROGGY) Oh, I'm feeling so relaxed. So much better now.*

DICK: *Good, maybe now we can talk about a payment schedule.*

MARTY: *Good-bye to all schedules, all responsibilities...*

DICK: *You can't just walk away from this debt.*

MARTY: *(SLURRING) Good-bye...good-bye to everyone...you'll miss me when I'm gone.*

VICTOR: *Gone? Gone where?*

MARTY: *Urghhh...things are getting dark.*

DICK: *Oh my God! Marty! What did you take!?*

MARTY: *It's...all...fading...away...one... less...insignificant... being...on...the...planet...*

DICK: *Marty? Marty!?*

MARTY: *Good-bye...cruel..wooorrrrllld...*

SFX: **THUMP ON FLOOR**

DICK: *Marty! Don't go! We'll settle for ten cents on the dollar. Marty...*

(CLICK!)

CHAPTER TWENTY-FIVE

The Alien Abduction Deception

MR. DICK CALLS LOUIE

SFX: ALIEN SPACESHIP.

LOUIE: *Hello. Can you hear me?*

DICK: *Uh yes, I can hear you.*

LOUIE: *I can't believe I'm getting reception this far out.*

DICK: *This far out?*

LOUIE: *Of the solar system. I must be at least twenty million miles from Earth. I'm glad I got Sprint.*

EDWIN: *What are you, kidding me? You expect me to believe that?*

LOUIE: *Listen, it's even hard for me to believe.*

DICK: *Oh, so you've been abducted by aliens.*

LOUIE: *Now you've got the picture.*

DICK: *Space aliens. Little green men?*

LOUIE: *I can't tell their sex, but most of them look like Dick Cheney.*

DICK: *Mr. Rogers, that's not going to fly around here.*

LOUIE: *Oh, this spaceship can fly anywhere. Even underwater. I was kidnapped right out of my Jacuzzi.*

DICK: *So let me get this straight. You're now on a flying saucer.*

LOUIE: *It's not really a saucer, it's more like, I don't know, a Volvo.*

DICK: *And for that reason, you are unable to pay your debt to Trans-Continental Savings and Loan. The credit we advanced you in good faith based on your promise to meet your obligations in a timely manner.*

LOUIE: *I couldn't have said it better myself.*

SFX: **ALIEN VOICES**

DICK: *Who's that?*

LOUIE: *I don't know. They haven't introduced themselves. But they seem to be holding some kind of medical instrument. Looks like a tube.*

DICK: *Mr. Rogers, all I want to know is when we can expect a check.*

LOUIE: *Speaking of which, they're checking me. All over the place. Even my --*

DICK: *Spare me the details, Mr. Rogers. I don't know your mental condition and frankly, I don't care. But even insanity is no defense for being financially in arrears.*

LOUIE: *That's where they are -- in my rear!*

DICK: *I've had it with you. I've had it with all this crap. You have till 3:00 PM.*

LOUIE: *Earth time?*

DICK: *Yes, Earth time! Because at 3:00 PM I'm going to refer you to our collection department. Then the matter will be totally out of my hands. At 3:00 PM we'll start calling your employer, your neighbors, your relatives, your friends, anyone and everyone in your whole miserable life. Do I make myself clear?*

LOUIE: *Perfectly. And when you call them, could you please tell them where I am. I've been having a little trouble getting through.*

(CLICK!)

REMEMBER!
All sound effects are available for free download at:
www.funnyguy.com/sfx

Or if you prefer, you may purchase
the SOUND EFFECTS CD at:
www.funnyguy.com/shop.htm

CHAPTER TWENTY-SIX

The Stable Relationship Ruse

MR. DICK CALLS SCOTT

SCOTT: *Who is it now?*

DICK: *This is mr Dick. I'm looking for Scott Crenshaw.*

SCOTT: *Go away, I don't want to speak to anybody. I'm too depressed.*

DICK: *About your financial situation?*

SCOTT: *No, about Agnes.*

DICK: *Agnes?*

SFX: **HORSE NEIGHING**

SCOTT: *She's so beautiful. So magnificent. And now she wants nothing to do with me. Absolutely nothing!*

DICK: *It sounds like you're in a stable.*

SCOTT: *Are you calling our home a stable!?*

DICK: *No, no, look. I just want you to realize you're in a bad situation.*

SCOTT: *Thanks to Agnes. I tried talking some plain old-fashioned horse sense into her, but she just kicks me out.*

DICK: *Of the house?*

SCOTT: *Of the stall!*

SFX: **HORSE SNORTING**

DICK: *Uh, this is very unusual, to say the least. But the bad situation I was referring was your credit balance.*

SCOTT: *I wanted to make it work. I wanted to have a stable relationship.*

DICK: *I'm sure you did. However, about your outstanding balance...*

SCOTT: *When I think of it, how we used to make hay.*

DICK: *This is all very interesting but the bank--*

SFX: **HORSE SQUEALING**

SCOTT: *You've upset Agnes! She's very sensitive.*

DICK: *I'm sorry. I didn't mean to.*

SCOTT: *Down girl, down. Let me brush you. There. There. Everything is going to be all right.*

DICK:	*Mr. Crenshaw, I'm sure you and Agnes will work it out, somehow.*
SCOTT:	*Easy for you to say. The object of your affection isn't strutting around town all night long, shaking her tail at every stallion she sees!*
SFX:	**HORSE BLOWING**
DICK:	*Can we please get back to the matter at hand. I know your relationship with Agnes must be, uh, very frustrating. But certainly that's no excuse for failure to meet your obligations.*
SCOTT:	*Oh, did I mention, she won't even let me mount her anymore.*
DICK:	*Mr. Crenshaw, please.*
SCOTT:	*Do you know the last time I had a night in the saddle? Or rode bareback?*
SFX:	**HORSE SNORTING**
DICK:	*Mr. Crenshaw, this conversation is getting out of hand. You're obsessed with this animal.*
SCOTT:	*You called Agnes an animal!? She's much better bred than you are! I want you to apologize to her right now.*
DICK:	*What do you mean?*
SCOTT:	*I mean you're going to get down on all fours and beg her forgiveness.*
SFX:	**HORSE SQUEALING**

DICK: *Mr. Crenshaw – I will do no such thing!*

SCOTT: *Not another word! On your knees! DO YOU HEAR
           ME!? Before I come over there with a buggy whip!!
           There. There. Agnes...*

           (CLICK!)

CHAPTER TWENTY-SEVEN

The Roulette Wheel Deal

MR. DICK CALLS ETHYL

SFX: CASINO SOUNDS/ROULETTE WHEEL

ETHYL: *Hi.*

DICK: *Is this Ethyl Winslow?*

ETHYL: *You bet it is!*

DICK: *This is Mr Dick. I'm calling about your credit card account with our bank.*

ETHYL: *I'm glad you called. I have a complaint. I tried to get another stack of ten dollar chips, but they turned down my card. What gives?*

DICK: *Where are you?*

ETHYL: *In Vegas. Playing Roulette. Can't you hear the action in the background? Are you deaf?*

DICK: *Miss Winslow, surely you're aware that you're sixteen hundred dollars over your credit limit. Plus you haven't made a minimum payment in nine months.*

ETHYL: *That's great!*

DICK: *That you haven't made a payment in nine months?*

ETHYL: *No, that I hit black! Oh, I'm getting hot. I'm practically on fire!*

DICK: *Miss Winslow, you must pay this sixteen hundred dollars in addition to your monthly minimum payment to keep your account in good standing.*

ETHYL: *Yeah!!!! Even!! Don't worry buddy! In a few minutes I'll be able to pay off the whole damn account -- with interest!*

DICK: *I'm not sure it's a really good idea to risk your capital in this way. May I remind you, your first obligation is to the bank. Perhaps if you quit now, you would have enough funds to---*

ETHYL: *Unbelievable!!!! 22 Black! A 35 - 1 shot ! I am loaded!*

DICK: *Loaded? How loaded?*

ETHYL: *I must have twenty-thousand in chips in front of me.*

DICK: *Miss Winslow, you only owe the bank $3600. Perhaps you should set that amount aside.*

ETHYL: *What are you nuts! My fingers are magic tonight. The wheel is alive. It's communicating with me. I can feel it!*

DICK: *Miss Winslow, please...*

ETHYL: *Shut up, you loser. You're distracting me. Okay, I want five grand low on numbers 1-18. Plus give me five grand on the second column.*

DICK: *Miss Winslow, be reasonable!*

ETHYL: *Let me see. What's a good street bet? Oh yeah, I got it. Five grand on those three numbers.*

DICK: *Miss –*

ETHYL: *Plus five grand on 35 red. Man on man, I'm going to clean up. There's no doubt about it. My retirement is right here and right now! Spin that wheel baby, spin that wheel! Here it comes! Here it comes!!*

(SILENCE)

DICK: *Miss Winslow? Miss Winslow!? Miss Winslow!!?*

ETHYL: *Uh, sure you can't raise my credit limit? This time, I swear, it's a sure thing.*

(CLICK!)

CHAPTER TWENTY-EIGHT

The Smoke Alarm Stunt

MR. DICK CALLS JOHNNY

JOHNNY: *Good afternoon.*

DICK: *Good afternoon. Is this Johnny Pervis.*

JOHNNY: *Yes, it is.*

DICK: *May I call you Johnny?*

JOHNNY: *Yes, you may.*

DICK: *Johnny, this is Mr. Dick from Hartcore & Brace. We recently purchased your debt from Massachusetts Federal Savings.*

JOHNNY: *How can I help you, Mr. Dick?*

DICK: Actually, you can help yourself. For one time only, we will allow you to settle this debt for only 97% of the current balance. But payment has to be made by five PM today.

JOHNNY: I see. That's a very good offer.

SFX: **SMOKE ALARM**

DICK: What's that?

JOHNNY: Nothing. Nothing at all.

DICK: It sounds like a smoke alarm.

JOHNNY: It's nothing. You were saying.

DICK: Are you sure there's nothing burning?

JOHNNY: Well, I hope that's not the case. I mean, why have a smoke detector if it's going to go off when nothing's burning. Kind of defeats the purpose, don't you think?

DICK: So you're saying there is something burning?

JOHNNY: Just the house!

DICK: The house!

JOHNNY: Well, tomorrow they were going to cancel my fire insurance. Something about not paying the premiums. So I figure, what the hell? Let it burn to the ground. I need the cash anyway.

DICK: You're not serious?

JOHNNY: *(COUGHING) Smoke's getting a little intense, but nothing I can't handle.*

DICK: *You've got to call the fire department. This is crazy!*

JOHNNY: *What are you worrying about? I never much liked this house anyway. It's too cold and drafty. Besides, it has a mold problem. Ever see what mold can do to your sinuses? It's not a pretty picture.*

DICK: *Johnny, you're not well.*

JOHNNY: *Thanks to all that mold.*

DICK: *No Johnny, you have to listen to me. You have to get out of the house right now. Do you hear me? Right now!*

JOHNNY: *Be kind of hard. The downstairs is all smoldering. Window seems to be locked too.*

DICK: *Then break the window. Save yourself!*

JOHNNY: *Been a whole lot easier if you hadn't of called. Here I've been talking to you, when I should have been getting out! I suppose if I die, it's kind of your fault.*

DICK: *My fault? Oh please! No! No!!*

SFX: **FIRE ENGINES AND SIRENS**

JOHNNY: *Wait a second. I think them fire folks have arrived. Let me take a look. Well, I'll be damned. There they are. A whole bunch of them too.*

DICK: *Thank God!*

SFX:	**CHOPPING DOOR**

JOHNNY: *Looks like they're chopping the door down. Got them hoses going too. Could even save the place at this rate.*

DICK: *Johnny, I am so happy to hear that. Why don't I put this file away for now? You obviously have enough to worry about.*

JOHNNY: *(COUGHING) You sure? I don't want you to get into any trouble.*

DICK: *Don't worry about me. Just take it one day at a time, okay?*

JOHNNY: *Sounds like good advice.*

DICK: *Good-bye Johnny.*

JOHNNY: *Good-bye Mr. Dick. You're a real Life Saver!*

(CLICK!)

CHAPTER TWENTY-NINE

The Echo System Strategem

Next time obnoxious creditors call, make them feel like they're talking to themselves. This technique is a total no-brainer. It's also great for telemarketers and pesky ex-lovers. Best of all, NO SOUND EFFECTS ARE NEEDED!

MR. DICK CALLS RALPH

RALPH: *Hello.*

DICK: *This is Mr. Dick and I'd like to speak to Ralph Plunkett.*

RALPH: *This is Mr. Dick and I'd like to speak to Ralph Plunkett.*

DICK: *Excuse me. I said I'd like to speak to Ralph Plunkett.*

RALPH: *Excuse me. I said I'd like to speak to Ralph Plunkett.*

DICK: *Is this Ralph Plunkett?*

RALPH: *Is this Ralph Plunkett?*

DICK: *Listen Mr. Plunkett, I don't know what kind of sick game you're playing, but I'm not buying it.*

RALPH: *Listen Mr. Plunkett, I don't know what kind of sick game you're playing, but I'm not buying it.*

DICK: *We are going to refer this account out for collection by Thursday if we don't receive a payment.*

RALPH: *We are going to refer this account out for --*

DICK: *You can run Mr. Plunkett, but you can't hide from the legal system. We'll get a judgment in court.*

RALPH: *You can run Mr. Plunkett, but you can't hide...*

DICK: *Stop imitating me!*

RALPH: *...from the legal system. We'll get a judgment in court. Stop imitating me!*

DICK: *That's what I said.*

RALPH: *That's what I said.*

DICK: *You may think this is funny. You may think this is amusing. But you won't be laughing when we seize your accounts.*

RALPH: *You may think this is funny. You may think this is amusing. But you won't be laughing when we seize your accounts.*

DICK: *That's right. We know where your assets are.*

RALPH: *That's right. We know where your assets are.*

DICK: *I know you can hear me.*

RALPH: *I know you can hear me.*

DICK: *I know you understand the consequences of not taking immediate action to correct this matter. I know you appreciate the terrible difficulty you will face for the rest of your life trying to get a car loan or a mortgage. But I also know this, Mr. Plunkett. I know that when people take responsibility for their finances, when they finally own up to their sacred obligations, it feels as though a great burden has been lifted off their shoulders. They can hold their heads up high once again. They can become responsible and respected members of the community. Mr. Plunkett, won't you join me in renouncing your sinful ways. It's not too late to achieve fiscal salvation. We will work with you in every possible way to make your life one hundred percent debt-free. Just think of it! No more fear, no more anxiety. Just the eternal bliss of a heavenly credit rating. So what do you say, Mr. Plunkett, what do you say?*

RALPH: *Uh, could you please repeat that?*

(CLICK!)

CHAPTER THIRTY

The Dubious Dracula Effect

MR. DICK CALLS BORIS

SFX: **SPOOKY OLD CRYPT**

BORIS: *Good evening*

DICK: *Good evening. Have I reached the home of Boris Nocturno?*

BORIS: *Yes, you have.*

DICK: *This is Mr. Dick from The Mutual Loan Company. You know, I've been trying to reach you all day.*

BORIS: *That is often difficult.*

DICK: *Are you saying you work during the day?*

BORIS: *Quite the contrary, I sleep all day.*

DICK:	*What are you, some kind of dead beat?*
BORIS:	*In a manner of speaking.*
DICK:	*Listen Boris, you know why I'm calling. There's a financial matter we have to discuss.*
BORIS:	*But I have no finances. All my assets are...liquid.*
DICK:	*Boris, we're going to get our money.*
BORIS:	*You can't get blood out of a stone. Believe me, I've tried.*
DICK:	*Without a payment, we're going to report you to the credit bureaus.*
BORIS:	*Oh those words! It's like a stake through my heart!*
SFX:	**HOWLING**
DICK:	*What was that?*
BORIS:	*That was Trudy. She's restless tonight.*
DICK:	*Is Trudy your wife?*
BORIS:	*Indeed she is. We've been married an eternity.*
DICK:	*Really. How long?*
BORIS:	*Next week we'll be celebrating our 437th anniversary.*
DICK:	*Stop yanking my chain!*
BORIS:	*Everybody tells me the same thing.*

DICK: *Okay, let's back up. You're buried in debt.*

BORIS: *Not to mention dirt.*

DICK: *So you're out in the garden?*

BORIS: *No, I'm actually down in my basement.*

DICK: *I don't care where you are. Your credit rating is on the line, buddy boy. Sooner or later you're going to see the light.*

BORIS: *I certainly hope not.*

DICK: *Bernard, you're getting to be a real pain in the neck!*

BORIS: *How many times have I heard that before?*

SFX: **COFFIN LID OPENING**

DICK: *Wait a second. It sounds like you're going out.*

BORIS: *Just out drinking. Every night I go out drinking.*

DICK: *No wonder you can't meet your obligations. Frankly, your whole attitude about your debt really sucks!*

BORIS: *Precisely. In any event, I've got to fly. I've got to flap my wings and go. No use hanging around here anymore.*

DICK: *Boris, we're going to find you!*

BORIS: *Not if I find you first. By the way, what's your blood type?*

(CLICK!)

REMEMBER!
All sound effects are available for free download at:
www.funnyguy.com/sfx

Or if you prefer, you may purchase
the SOUND EFFECTS CD at:
www.funnyguy.com/shop.htm

CHAPTER THIRTY-ONE

The Fabulous Flute Fantasy

MR. DICK CALLS WILMA

SFX:　　**FLUTE PLAYING**

WILMA:　*House of Flutes.*

DICK:　*Does Wilma Parkinson live there?*

WILMA:　*That's her, on the flute.*

DICK:　*Could you possibly get her attention?*

WILMA:　*Is this an emergency?*

DICK:　*Kind of. I'm calling about an important business matter.*

SFX:　　**FLUTE DUO**

WILMA:　*Well, if you're selling flutes, we have quite enough already.*

DICK: *What do you mean?*

WILMA: *For the flute society. Wilma is the leader of our
          Flute Society.*

DICK: *Look, I'm sure that's a very prestigious position.
          But I really have to speak to her.*

WILMA: *So you're selling sheet music?*

DICK: *I have nothing to do with music!*

SFX: **MORE FLUTES**

WILMA: *Then why are you calling Wilma?*

DICK: *I told you why I was calling.*

WILMA: *Well, she's very busy. The Flute Society is preparing
          a five-day recital based on The Civil War. All original
          compositions.*

DICK: *That's fascinating. I just need Wilma for a few moments.*

SFX: **EVEN MORE FLUTES**

WILMA: *Hold it! Did you hear that?*

DICK: *If you would—*

WILMA: *That was The Battle of Gettysburg. I swear, it feels like
          I'm almost there: The Union and Confederate armies
          facing off against each other, all those handsome men in
          their uniforms. It makes me want to swoon!*

SFX: **LONE, HIGH-PITCHED FLUTE**

DICK: *What was that?*

WILMA: *Lincoln getting shot. They're carrying him out of the theatre. The nation is in shock!*

DICK: *Tell Wilma I must –*

WILMA: *What will we do without our President? How will we go on? How will the country survive!?*

DICK: *I know, I know, it's terrible what happened to Lincoln.*

WILMA: *Terrible? Terrible!? What do you mean terrible? It serves him right! That damn Yankee!!*

(CLICK!)

CHAPTER THIRTY-TWO

The Post-Pregnancy Plot

MR. DICK CALLS MARION

SFX: CRYING BABY

MARION: *Could you hold on a minute? I've got my hands full.*

DICK: *Okay.*

MARION: *Just a few seconds. Okay. Whew. That's better.*

(BABY STOPS CRYING)

DICK: *Is this Marion Wedgies?*

MARION: *Yes sir, this is her.*

DICK: *This is Mr. Dick. We've been trying to contact you concerning your account. But you haven't responded to our letters. And I've left numerous messages on your answering machine.*

SFX: **SECOND BABY CRYING**

MARION: *I can't believe this. Just hold on, okay?*

DICK: *Okay.*

MARION: *Come to mama. Mama has something good for you. That's right. Go ahead. Whew. Thank God I have two breasts.*

(SECOND BABY STOPS CRYING)

DICK: *I'm sorry. I didn't know you were breastfeeding. In fact, we didn't even know you were pregnant.*

MARION: *What's that supposed to mean?*

DICK: *Well, according to our records, you're sixty-seven.*

MARION: *Are you saying I'm too old to have children? That sounds a lot like age discrimination to me, young man!*

SFX: **TWO BABIES CRYING**

DICK: *No, no, I didn't mean it like that. I'm sorry.*

MARION: *Yeah, sure you are.*

DICK: *Really, I'm sorry.*

MARION: *Okay, I accept your apology.*

DICK: *Thank you. It sounds like you had twins.*

MARION: *Twins? I should be so lucky!*

SFX: **THREE BABIES CRYING**

DICK: *Hello? Hello? Are you still there?*

MARION: *Just hold on. We have a small problem here. Seems like little Susie can't wait her turn. Okay Herbie, you've had enough. Leave some for your sister. Herbie get off me!! Whew. What a pig he is! Just like his father!*

(THREE BABIES STOP CRYING)

DICK: *Uh, you had triplets?*

MARION: *I should be so lucky. Now where were we?*

DICK: *Umm...let me check my...um...*

MARION: *My account. You were talking about my account.*

DICK: *Right, right. There's just a small matter of six payments that are due. Now, I know this may be a bad time. But perhaps you could --*

SFX: **FOUR BABIES CRYING**

MARION: *It sounds like a day care center in here! Libby, I think you've had your fill. Let your brother Stevie have his turn. Young lady, your brother Stevie is waiting. Listen Libby, I'm not running a dairy farm over here!*

DICK: *On the other hand, maybe you could arrange...*

MARION: *Herbie! Susie! Libby! Stevie! Stop this crying this instant! I'm getting a migraine!!*

(FOUR BABIES STOP CRYING)

DICK: *...to have your husband--*

MARION: *What husband? Does it sound to you like I have a husband!? What are you trying to do? Rub it in!!? Is that the policy of your bank!?*

DICK: *No, no, no. I'm sorry I called. Believe me, it won't happen again.*

MARION: *Sure it won't.*

DICK: *Really and truly, I won't call.*

MARION: *You'll have to prove it, buster. Starting right now!*

DICK: *Okay, okay, I promise. You'll never hear from me again. Have a nice day. And, uh, congratulations...*

(CLICK!)

CHAPTER THIRTY-THREE

The Highly Questionable Approach

Creditors love to ask you questions. Why not ask them questions? Questions that will drive them insane. What kind of questions, you may ask? Don't worry, we have plenty of them right here. This example will help you learn this invaluable technique. NO SOUND EFFECTS NEEDED!

MR. DICK CALLS QUENTIN

QUENTIN: *Who do you want?*

DICK: *I want Quentin Frasier?*

QUENTIN: *Why?*

DICK: *I have a private business matter to discuss with him.*

QUENTIN: *What kind of business?*

DICK: *I can only discuss that with him. Is this him?*

QUENTIN: *Well, I can only discuss that with you. That is, if you are you?*

DICK: *What do you mean if I am I?*

QUENTIN: *What do you think I mean?*

DICK: *This is getting us nowhere.*

QUENTIN: *Where else would you like to go?*

DICK: *Listen, stop trying to evade the issue.*

QUENTIN: *What issue?*

DICK: *The issue we were taking about.*

QUENTIN: *Which was?*

DICK: *Quentin Frasier. Is this Quentin Frasier? Just answer yes or no?*

QUENTIN: *Why should I answer just yes or no?*

DICK: *I'm the one asking the questions here!*

QUENTIN: *Why's that?*

DICK: *I'm getting very tired of this.*

QUENTIN: *You are?*

DICK: *Yes, I am. I'm going to cut to the chase. If this is Quentin Frasier, you must call the law office of Dickey and Doogan before 1:00 PM.*

QUENTIN: *Pacific Standard Time?*

DICK: *No, No, Eastern Standard Time!*

QUENTIN: *Why's that?*

DICK: *Because Dickey and Doogan are in Philadelphia!*

QUENTIN: *How long have they been in Philadelphia?*

DICK: *Twenty-seven years.*

QUENTIN: *Where were they before that?*

DICK: *I have nothing further to say to you!*

QUENTIN: *Are you sure?*

(CLICK!)

CHAPTER THIRTY-FOUR

The Downtown Jail Jest

MR. DICK CALLS PHILIP

SFX: **LOCK-UP - CELL DOORS - CHAINS**
SHOUTS - ETC

PHILIP: *Central Booking*

DICK: *Excuse me?*

PHILIP: *I said Central Booking. Who do you want?*

DICK: *Uh, Phillip Vanderhoff.*

PHILIP: *This his lawyer?*

DICK: *No, this is Mr. Dick, a business associate.*

PHILIP: *Look pal, you got to be more specific. What's he in for?*

DICK: *In for?*

PHILIP: *Yeah, what's he done? What's the rap sheet on him?*

DICK: *I'm calling because Mr. Vanderhoff has an outstanding balance.*

PHILIP: *Come again?*

DICK: *On his credit card.*

PHILIP: *You're kidding me, right? This is a joke, right?*

DICK: *No, I'm very serious*

PHILIP: *What are you, hallucinating? We got murderers, thieves, rapists, drug dealers down here and you want to speak to someone about their credit card.*

DICK: *If it wouldn't be too much trouble.*

SFX: **ALARMS**

PHILLIP: *Damn! Some animal got out of his cage. We're in total lockdown.*

DICK: *Is that bad?*

PHILIP: *It'll be bad for the slob who's trying to escape, once we get him in our sights.*

DICK: *Dear Lord!*

PHILIP: *Let's get back to this Phillip character. You got a description? Tall, short, husky, Caucasian, Asian, what?*

DICK: *Why do you need a description?*

PHILIP: *Hey buddy, I got fifty of these clowns in a holding pen, and they ain't been processed yet. So work with me here.*

DICK: *Okay, let's see. He's thirty-two years old and I think Caucasian and –*

SFX: **GUN SHOTS**

PHILIP: *They nailed him! Right between the eyes!*

DICK: *Dear Lord!*

PHILIP: *Yeah, some pieces of scum never learn their lesson. Where were we?*

DICK: *Uh, Phillip Vanderhoff.*

PHILIP: *Thirty-two, right?*

DICK: *Right*

PHILIP: *Caucasian, right?*

DICK: *I believe so.*

PHILIP: *Well, you're in luck. We only got one guy down here that fits that description.*

DICK: *Great.*

PHILIP: *The guy we just shot. Where should we ship the body?*

(CLICK!)

CHAPTER THIRTY-FIVE

The Self-Analysis Set-Up

There's nothing wrong with being a neurotic mess. Particularly, when you find yourself dealing with creditors. With your inner world being such a disaster, how can they possibly expect you to deal with the real world. In this approach, you WON'T need sound effects. Just be your normal insecure self!

MR. DICK CALLS NATHAN

NATHAN: *Hello.*

DICK: *My name is Mr. Dick. I'm looking for Nathan Rogers.*

NATHAN: *Me too.*

DICK: *You mean he's not there?*

NATHAN: *No, he's here.*

DICK: *If he's there, could you please put him on.*

NATHAN: *He is on.*

DICK: *You mean you're the Nathan Rogers I'm looking for.*

NATHAN: *No. I'm the Nathan Rogers I'm looking for. The real Nathan Rogers. That genuine, sweet, sensitive soul that I know exists beneath this coarse, cynical, irresponsible exterior.*

DICK: *Can we cut to the chase?*

NATHAN: *That's it exactly. I've been chasing Nathan Rogers in all the wrong places. How many times have I tried to actualize the authentic Nathan Rogers in therapy? How many seminars have I taken in self-fulfillment? How many times have I gotten myself hypnotized to create that vision of --*

DICK: *This is not getting us anywhere.*

NATHAN: *You are so perceptive! All of it didn't get me anywhere. Twenty-five years of trying to find the very essence of Nathan Rogers and then, all of a sudden, I located him.*

DICK: *Where was he?*

NATHAN: *Alaska.*

DICK: *But you live in Cincinnati.*

NATHAN: *Precisely my point. By the time I got there, he was gone.*

DICK: *As I said, I don't think this is getting us anywhere.*

NATHAN: *Where do you want to get?*

DICK: *I want to get to Nathan Rogers! I want to get to Nathan Rogers right now!*

NATHAN: *Of course you do. Me too.*

(CLICK!)

CHAPTER THIRTY-SIX

The Pile Driver Predicament

MR. DICK CALLS SCOTT

SCOTT: *Hello.*

DICK: *I have an urgent call for Scott Anderson. Is this Scott Anderson?*

SCOTT: *It always has been.*

DICK: *Scott, I'd like to offer you an opportunity. A once in a lifetime opportunity. An opportunity you absolutely cannot afford to walk away from.*

SCOTT: *Sounds good.*

FRANK: *As I'm checking your file, I see that your combined outstanding balance is $7365.12? Is that correct?*

SCOTT: *To the penny.*

DICK: *The truth is, we want to avoid litigation whenever we can. We want to create win-win situations.*

SCOTT: *So do I.*

DICK: *I'm very pleased to hear that, Scott. Therefore I'd like to present to you a very attractive settlement offer.*

SCOTT: *Let's hear it.*

SFX: **PILE DRIVER**

DICK: *If you agree to pay 85% of the entire balance by 12:00 PM, we will consider the matter closed.*

SCOTT: *Could you repeat that? And speak a little louder. They're working outside.*

SFX: **CONSTRUCTION SOUNDS - HAMMERING, ETC**

DICK: *I said, pay 85% of the entire balance by--*

SCOTT: *Wait, wait. I can hardly hear you.*

DICK: *PAY 85% OF THE ENTIRE BALANCE BY 3:00 PM AND WE WILL--*

SCOTT: *You're just not coming through.*

SFX: **PILE DRIVERS & CONSTRUCTION SOUNDS**

DICK: *I'M SCREAMING MY LUNGS OUT OVER HERE!*

SCOTT: *Well, don't yell at me. I have no control over those construction guys.*

DICK: *WHEN WOULD BE A GOOD TIME TO CALL BACK!?*

SCOTT: *Let's see. They should be finished in about two years.*

DICK: *TWO YEARS!?*

SCOTT: *Believe me, it's a real headache. I'm got to deal with this seven days a week. They're building three hundred condos next door. And a stadium!*

DICK: *THAT'S INSANE!!*

(CONSTRUCTION SOUNDS STOP)

SCOTT: *Whew. What a relief. Now could you please repeat what you were saying?*

DICK: *It'll be a pleasure. If you agree to pay 85% of the entire balance by --*

SFX: **PILE DRIVERS & CONSTRUCTION SOUNDS**

SCOTT: *Excuse me. Could you please speak up?*

(CLICK!)

WHO IS FUNNYGUY.COM?

David Samson is a nationally known speaker, media guest, and the author of twenty-one books. His published works include: *The Joy of Depression; Men Who Hate Themselves (And The Women Who Agree With Them); American Idle; Wake Up and Smell The Coffin; How To Get God To Return Your Calls; The Middle Age Of Aquarius; Useless Knowledge; Masturbation For Morons; The Official Millennium Survival Handbook;* plus *Do Reality Checks Ever Bounce?*

In self-help psychology, he's written: *Love Codes, 1001 Ways You Reveal Your Personality, 1001 More Ways You Reveal Your Personality; Parents Who Stay Lovers; Is He For Real?* and *Is He Mr. Right?* David also wrote *Telling It My Way with Tammy Faye Bakker* and *The Post Pregnancy Workout with Rob Parr* (the trainer of Madonna, Demi Moore, Maria Shriver, etc).

His books have been seen on *David Letterman, The Today Show, Rosie 'O' Donnell, Regis and Kathy Lee, Geraldo Rivera, Politically Incorrect, ABC Prime Time Live, FOX Morning News, Comedy Central, Entertainment Tonight, Donahue,* and *Larry King.* He's also a frequent guest on major radio shows including top ten affiliate markets of *ABC, CBS, FOX, Clear Channel, Westwood One, Radio America,* and *Pacifica Broadcasting.*

His work has been featured or he has been interviewed in *People, Penthouse, Cosmopolitan, The New York Daily News, The Chicago Tribune, The Christian Science Monitor, The Philadelphia Metro, USA Today, Los Angeles Magazine,* plus *The New York Times.*

David Samson is a professional member of the **National Speakers Association**. He's been a Creative Executive at some of America's largest advertising agencies, and often consults with clients in that area.

He gives himself lots of CREDIT!

If you cannot get our titles at your local bookstore they're available at:

funnyguy.com

and at

spibooks.com

☐ THE JOY OF DEPRESSION
by David Samson

Depression is much more than a state-of-mind. It's a total way of living! And the perfect way to cope with all the stress of modern life. Learn the secrets of financial insecurity. Project negative charisma. Overcome the effects of a healthy childhood! Plus always remember: The best years of your life are still behind you!   **$11.95**

☐ MEN WHO HATE THEMSELVES
— AND THE WOMEN WHO AGREE WITH THEM
by David Samson

Here's the truth about Living, Loving, and Loathing! Why men suffer from PMS (Pre-Marital Syndrome). What "The Male Lie-Bido" has to say. Plus advice from Dr. Baby Ruth; Buy-Sexuality in Women; Aero-Phobics for Men; Impersonal Ads; and much more!   **$11.95**

☐ WAKE UP AND SMELL THE COFFIN
by David Samson

Are you reading Chicken Soup for the Departed Soul? Is Weed Killer now more important than Killer Weed? Has LSD come to mean Low Sodium Diet? Have you joined a 12 Step Program just to get up twelve steps? Are the Grateful Dead friends of yours who've visited Dr. Kevorkian? Then congratulations! This is the right book for you!   **$11.95**

☐ AMERICAN IDLE
THE ANTI-MOTIVATION HANDBOOK
by David Samson

Make "Positive Thinking" a thing of the past! David Samson is "The Master of Poor Performance." Martha Stewart and Donald Trump haven't consulted with him — but you should! So overcome feelings of optimism! Achieve the stagnation you deserve! And remember those two little words that will forever set you free: WHY BOTHER?   **$11.95**

☐ THE O'REALLY FACTOR
by David Samson

Bill O' Really is always right— far right! But he loves to spread liberal doses of humor around. On this CD hear him rant about: Al Gore, Al Qaeda, The ACLU, UCLA, The Homeless, The Vacation Homeless, Gay Marriage, Gay Divorce, Health Insurance, Wealth Insurance, Operators in India, Operators in Indiana, and much more! Tune into The O' Really Factor today. It's totally unfair and unbalanced!   **$11.95**

☐ IS HE FOR REAL?
Knowing Sooner What A Man Will Be Like Later
by David Samson and Dr. Elayne Kahn

Separate the cream from the creeps! Because here, using the same methods as FBIprofilers, men's secret signals about love and romance are finally exposed! This powerful and amusing book is spiced with intimate details. Know exactly what kind of lover he is — before going to bed. Now get the love you desire -- the love you deserve!   **$12.95**

☐ IS HE MR. RIGHT?
How To tell If You Should Love Him or Leave Him
by David Samson and Dr. Elayne Kahn

Is he ready to commit — or should he be committed? Does he want to build a relationship — or tear you down? Should you wed him or shed him? This fact-filled manual picks up where "Is He For Real? leaves off. Is He Mr. Right? It would be wrong to buy any other book to find out!   **$12.95**

HOW TO GET GOD TO RETURN YOUR CALLS
by David Samson

Feeling disconnected from God? Suspect your calls never even go through? Paranoid about being snubbed at the Heavenly Level? Well, worry no longer! Learn how to access God's private line. Cut through Cosmic Clutter and top His "Must Get Back To Immediately" list. Hundreds of proven techniques to get the answers you deserve! **$11.95**

MASTURBATION FOR MORONS
A DO-IT-YOURSELF HANDBOOK
by David Samson

The very first book for Mono-Sexuals! Find out why two people are one person too many. How to be your own best lover. The issue of Mono-Sexual marriage. Avoiding stains on your reputation. What to do when things get out of hand. Stiffening your resolve in the face of adversity. Yes, this is one handbook you won't be able to put down! **$11.95**

DO REALITY CHECKS EVER BOUNCE?
by David Samson
Illustrated by Martin Archer

Is your inner child adopted? Can white trash be recycled? Do cold fronts have warm behinds? Should liver transplants come with onions? Obviously, these can't be answered by any person -- any sane person! Plus each outrageous page is hilariously illustrated. You won't be able to stop laughing! **$9.95**

THE OFFICIAL MILLENNIUM SURVIVAL HANDBOOK
by David Samson and Peter Bergman

You're not out of the woods yet! Find out what you need to know all way up to the year 2999. Because the new Millennium will be an equal opportunity annihilator. Lawyers, arsonists, dentists will all find themselves in the same boat as you -- namely the Titanic! Written with Peter Bergman of the legendary Firesign Theater! **$9.95**

DEAR READER:

If you liked (or disliked) this book, please review the following pages for descriptions and ordering information on the other fine works in this series!

Funnyguy.com books are available in select bookstores around the world. If you can't get them at your favorite local bookshop, please use the order form that is provided. On U.S. orders that you mail in or fax, we will pay the shipping! On orders outside of the U.S., please add shipping of: $5.95 for the first book and $1.00 for each added book.

Thank You!

The Publisher

Get The Entire

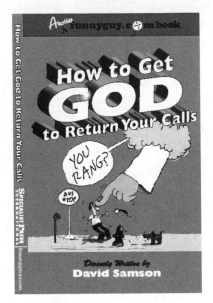

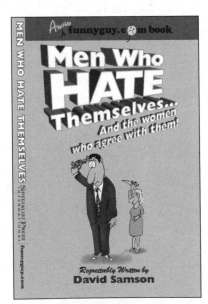

Funnyguy.com Library!

143

SPECIALIST PRESS
INTERNATIONAL
and
funnyguy.c☺m books

Our titles are available in local bookstores. If you cannot order them locally,
you can get them online at: funnyguy.com or spibooks.com,
by fax: 212- 431-8646 or by phone: 212-431-5011

IF PAYING WITH CREDIT CARD: (CIRCLE ONE): VISA   MC   AMEX

NAME ON CARD: _____

CARD HOLDER SIGNTURE – ABOVE

CARD'S 3 OR 4 DIGIT #
(USUALLY ON BACK): _____

CARD #: _____   **EXP DATE:** _____

CREDIT CARD BILLING ADDRESS: **SHIPPING ADDRESS FOR YOUR ORDER:**

Email us your order to:
sales@spibooks.com
by entering the data above and sending it to us. Email orders don't need signatures.
Snail mail address: SPI BOOKS • 99 Spring St. • NY, NY • 10012
Make checks payable to: SPI Books

(Please Xerox this order form if you elect to mail or fax us your order)

QTY	ISBN	TITLE	PRICE
	978-156171-211-3	The Joy of Depression	$11.95
	978-156171-825-2	How To Get God To Return Your Calls	$11.95
	978-156171- 826-9	Men Who Hate Themselves And The Women Who Agree With Them	$11.95
	978-156171-827-6	American Idle	$11.95
	978-156171- 213-7	Wake Up and Smell The Coffin	$11.95
	978-156171-214-4	The O'Really Factor	$11.95
	978-156171-217-5	Masturbation For Morons	$11.95
	978-156171-216-8	How To Be Funny When You Owe Money	$11.95
	156171-985-4	Is He For Real?	$12.95
	156171-912-9	Is He Mr. Right?	$12.95
	156171-995-1	The Official Post Millenium Handbook	$9.95
	156171-998-6	Do Reality Checks Ever Bounce?	$9.95
Total Enclosed:			$
Tax in NY State:			$
GRAND TOTAL:			$